So You Want

to Play College Baseball?

131 Things Every Ball Player Needs to Know About College Baseball

by Dan Green

RoseDog❦Books

PITTSBURGH, PENNSYLVANIA 15238

RoseDog Books
585 Alpha Drive
Pittsburgh, PA 15238
Visit our website at www.bookstore.dorrancepublishing.com

ISBN: 978-1-4809-8365-6
eISBN: 978-1-4809-8342-7

This book is dedicated to the game of baseball. It has taught me so much about life and I know it has shaped the lives of many others who have come before me. May baseball continue to shape and teach not only our youth, but all people of life's lessons. May all those who currently or have ever played, coached, or been a fan of this game help keep America's pastime alive and well.

To all those who love this game, the greatest game in the world – may baseball never die.

1. The Coach's Office is a Sacred Place

All player or coach meetings will take place in the coach's office. The majority of college baseball coaches will meet with captains, coaches, and players individually in this space and when entering the coach's office you should be awake and prepared to talk about anything, especially grades, team chemistry, or individual performance. All coaches are different but most have an "open door" policy and welcome you to stop in just to say "hello" or to ask any questions you may have. Communicating with the coach in person is the best way to establish and maintain an effective relationship between player and coach.

2. The Differences Between DI, DII, DIII, & JuCos

DI - There are roughly 300 Division I college baseball programs in the United States. The NCAA has set the maximum DI baseball roster size at 35 players in the regular season and 25 baseball players during the playoffs. DI players are expected to produce and some DI players will go on to play professional baseball. Keep this in mind when choosing a school and being serious about your future in collegiate or professional baseball. Red Shirts exists.

DII - There are roughly 300 Division II college baseball programs in the United States. Typically, these are smaller public and private schools with under 10,000 students. These schools can give partial scholarships for student athletes, but rarely does a DII program have enough money to give any one player a "Full ride." Most DII players could play at the Division I level, but decided to play DII for more playing time and/or a better scholarship package.

DIII - There are roughly 400 Division III college baseball programs in the United States. These schools cannot provide prospects with any "athletic" money or scholarships, but can provide all students with financial aid packages, based on student's academic performance and standings. These packages vary from college to college, but financial aid at DIII schools cannot be any different for athletes as they are available for the general student body. Additionally, students cannot "Redshirt*" for medical, athletic, or academic purposes.

JuCo - "Juco" is the commonly used slang word for junior college. These are two year institutions. Junior Colleges are allotted 12 scholarships each season. There are 473 junior colleges that offer baseball as a varsity sport.

*Redshirting - when an athlete is held out of competition for a season in order to develop the athlete's skills and extend their period of playing eligibility

3. The Truth about Scholarships

Each DI college baseball program is allotted 11.7 scholarships, as of the 2018 season. Each DI program may split these 11.7 scholarships among 27 different players. It is very rare that a high school student is offered a full athletic scholarship at a Division I college. For many high school baseball players this is the dream, but for many high school baseball players this will not be the reality. A full scholarship covers tuition, fees, books, room and board, supplies, and sometimes living expenses. DI colleges offering an athlete a scholarship based on athletic ability must give that student at least 25% or more of a full scholarship.

Each DII college baseball program is allotted nine scholarships per season. DII programs tend to split their scholarships into quarter scholarships for each athlete and will rarely, if ever, provide an athlete with a "full ride."

There are no athletic scholarships for Division III schools, but the school still provides financial aid to those academically eligible.

Each junior college is allotted with 12 scholarships per season.

4. College Baseball is not for Everyone

This is one of the most simple concepts, yet people won't understand this idea. College athletics requires a ridiculously high level of dedication and commitment to your sport. Some players will not play all 4 years that they have eligibility for a variety of different reasons. Regardless of the sport, life is harder and more is required of you in a shorter amount of time than the average student. If having a lot of free time is important to you or you have a stronger passion than your sport, you will likely find yourself letting baseball go during your college years. College baseball is not for everyone.

5. Walking On and Trying Out

If you are a player looking to walk onto a team or try out to make a roster there are a few details you must be aware of. If the program has dedicated athletic scholarships to players it is almost certain those players will make the team, even if they struggle mightily in tryouts. There is nothing wrong with walking on or trying out for a team. Each college coach makes his roster based on a different process, but knowing the process and how you will be evaluated is important to know prior to starting the tryout. Don't be afraid to ask questions and get as many specific details about the tryout as possible directly from the head coach.

6. Recruiting Visits

I can't stress the importance of this enough. Don't sit behind a computer screen clicking around to decide your future. If you are interested in a school, go check it out in person and meet the baseball coach. The first impression you make on a coach will have a huge impact on your future. Visualize how you see your recruiting visit going and make it happen.

7. Meeting the Coach

Step one: Make and maintain eye contact with any coach you meet.

Step two: Firm handshake - no worse way to meet someone than to give them a "dead fish" handshake.

Step three: Smile - even if you're nervous and feel like you might lose your lunch. It will go a long way to calming you down and showing your excitement and enthusiasm. The rest will take care of itself.

8. Student Athlete

Student will always come first. You'll be a student and incur all the responsibilities and expectations of being a student, as well as being on an athletic team regardless of what division you play at.

9. Bus Rides

You will learn to love these and embrace being a "road warrior." The only way to get through college baseball is to love the time spent with your teammates because baseball is a sport with a lot of down time. These bus rides will be a staple to your adventure that is college baseball and I recommend leaving the headphones in your room and spending the time on the road talking or playing games on the bus with your friends. Pack different clothing options in case the bus is too hot or cold, along with your pregame snack of choice.

10. The Locker Room

The locker room physically looks different for every team, but there are some locker rooms that are "closer" than others. This is the team's own personal space which may be the location for anything from dance parties to postseason celebrations to team meetings or even player fights.

11. The Trainer's Room

The perception of the trainer's room is different for everyone. Some players will never go into the athletic trainer's room even if they are hurt or need help because they do not want to be labeled as "soft." Other players have no problem turning to their athletic trainers for help when needed and don't think any more or any less of those players who use these services. These players go to athletic training before and after every practice, scrimmage, or game to stretch and do the exercises that are going to help their performance and keep them healthy throughout the season. I would recommend using these resources. The team trainer is a qualified medical staff member who is there to keep you healthy and performing at your best. Additionally, the room and facility itself are there to help you improve and recover. Use these valuable resources that are available to you such as the ice bath, stationary bike, etc.

12. Cafeteria Food

It is very difficult to fuel your body with the necessary dietary requirements it takes to be an "elite" athlete. Many times the food options and college cafeteria upsets many students' stomachs and does not offer food that will lead to optimal performance. Be prepared to buy protein bars, protein powders, nutrition bars, and any other food that you need to have the energy and fuel to perform at your best even if it means an additional out of pocket cost to you or your parents.

13. The Shortened Season

The high school season runs roughly from March to early June. The collegiate season runs roughly from mid-February to early-June at the DI level. In DII and DIII, the season runs from March to early May. Obviously, the ending date depends on how far your team goes at both the high school and collegiate levels, but you can expect the season to come and go in the blink of an eye. You will dedicate 12 months to your college baseball season if you are a serious player, yet the season will last about two and a half or maybe three months if you are on a good team. For a dedicated starting pitcher, that might mean training anywhere from 300 to 365 days a year for a total of six to twelve starts. For a position player in the starting line-up, you are looking at roughly 80 to 100 at bats depending on your production and where you are batting in the lineup.

14. Transitioning from Seven Inning Games to Nine Inning Games

Most high school players don't understand the importance of this change. First of all, this requires an entire extra hour of focus each game. Also, this reveals the importance of having a full, quality bullpen. In high school if your team had one or two top notch starting pitchers your team could win many games and have a successful season because these studs could just pitch and dominate an entire game. Now in college, your bullpen is required to be just as effective as your starting pitchers. There is no worse feeling for a pitcher or a team when the starter goes seven or eight strong innings and the bullpen blows the game and the team leaves the field with an "L".

15. Conference Games and Rivals

You will learn about these conference rivals no matter where you go to college and no matter what level you play at. These opponents will decide the fate of your season, year after year after year. Rivalries between players and between teams brew throughout a player's four year career at a school. You will realize that being in the line-up or pitching in a conference game means the coach trusts you more than the players not in the game. This is the ultimate goal because these games mean the most. Non-conference games are still important for regional and national rankings. However, to end the season with the best conference record will give your team the top seed in the conference tournament. For example, if a team finishes 17-13 overall, but their conference record is 4-13, they would likely not make their conference tournament even though their overall record is 17-13. Contrastly, if a team goes 17-13 with a conference record of 17-0, they would likely make the conference tournament as the 1 seed. With that said, you want to be in the lineup when you play your conference opponents.

16. Double Headers

In general, these double headers tend to happen on the weekend, but the new part about these days for you will be the length. If you have an away double header, your bus could leave at 7:00 am, to get the team there at 9:00 am, in time to prepare for a 10:00 am start. Game 1 can last 3 hours easily which takes us to 1:00pm. Then, both teams likely will be given 30 minutes to eat lunch and regroup for a 1:30pm start of Game 2. Another 3 hour game would bring us to 4:30pm. Next, your team will get back on the bus for another 2 hours to get you home. This example gets you back to the locker room at 6:30pm. Remember, your team left 7:00 am this morning. You must be committed to play this sport and double headers will weed out who is committed to 12 hour baseball days and who is not. Now these are just rough estimates. Sometimes games go into extra innings or last longer than 3 hours and sometimes a pitcher throws a "no-hitter" that can last an hour. In general, don't make any plans on double header days.

17. Playing Time

This is earned. No one is guaranteed any regardless of seniority or circumstance. If you don't like it, play better.

18. Seniority

This is something most people learn the hard way. As it relates to depth charts, captain's status, and popularity, seniority some-what applies to all these situations. A returning player, oftentimes, knows more and has experienced more college baseball than you.

19. Girls

Sometimes a college will have a group of girls that love to follow the baseball team. These girls are called "cleat chasers." Other times, many individual girls will like or have certain attractions to baseball players and follow them or the team on their own. Any college athlete has an unfair advantage over the average student with the majority of girls. Whether you like attention or hate attention, you can expect it when you decide to become a collegiate athlete at any level.

20. Parties

Now, everyone's college experience is different. You may be a player who never spends time with his team outside of the baseball field, but more likely than not you will be friends with your teammates off the field as well. Some baseball programs have certain traditions they uphold and some don't. The quicker you learn about the party scene at your school and within your team, the more comfortable you will be choosing how you spend your free time. Each institution has its own rules on consequences for underage drinking, drug use, etc. These consequences can be as strict as losing scholarship money, being removed from your athletic team, or even being expelled from your school.

21. Politics

Just like in every aspect of life, there are always politics. Maybe a coach will continue to play a struggling player just because the program has given him an athletic scholarship to play baseball at your college. Maybe a coach has been family friends with the father of a player who is on the team and he is being given unfair or unwarranted chances to perform. As frustrating and as unfair as this is you will learn that life is not fair either. Life is 10% what happens to you and 90% how you react to it. Have the guts to change your approach at the plate, learn a new position, or develop a new pitch. Do whatever it takes, within the rules, to get yourself on the field.

22. Team Lifts

Every program has a different strength and conditioning program, but the team will likely have organized lifts. It is proven that all people are stronger together than apart. Athletes can move more weight when they are working in front of teammates than when they are working individually at the gym. Some programs have 5:00 am or 6:00 am team lifts before the classes start. Some colleges have their team lifts year-round, some don't. We know every college is different, but the moral of the story here is be prepared to commit your life to this dream.

23. Lack of Food Choices

As previously mentioned, the cafeteria is not always the athlete's best friend. Some cafeteria's best options are pizza, soda, and other unhealthy food choices. The stigma of college for most males can be described in two words: pizza and beer. Although this is merely a stereotype, many people actually end up falling in love with this diet as a lifestyle, which obviously can lead to poor academic and athletic performance. Break the stereotype and find nutritious foods. Your body and performance will thank you.

24. The College Athlete's Priorities

God/Religion/Faith, Family, School, Sports, Friends, Boyfriends/Girlfriends. This list comes in no specific order, but these words were the most frequently used to describe college baseball players' top priorities.

25. Layers!

You can always take it off, but if you don't bring it, you can't wear it. This especially applies for pitchers and bench players! Always be prepared for any weather! Wind, snow, rain, sun, etc. Be overly prepared with bug spray, sunscreen, sunglasses, Chapstick, rain-proof gear, etc.

26. Time Management

This might be the most important skill you will learn as a college baseball player. When you have what feels like an insane amount of things to do and no time to do it, you start deciding just how important things are to you. Your first year will be the hardest year for this reason, but once you figure out how to get everything done that you need to get done, it gets easier and becomes a habit. It is all about balancing academics, athletics, and social life.

27. Do the Little Things Right On and Off the Field

I'm sure by now everyone has been told the importance of the little things. The difference between winning and losing can be one simple little thing like backing up a base or getting a bunt down. Once you carry this mentality into your life outside of baseball is when you shift from a boy to a man.

Do the thing little things right on and off the field - even when you don't feel like it. Get the bunt down. Back up the base. Back up the throws to the pitcher every pitch. Take the time to send your mom a card on Mother's Day. Give your little sibling a call just to say, "What's up?" Doing the little things will change your life and let others know how much they mean to you.

28. College Baseball's Life Lessons

Baseball is the greatest sport of all time because it teaches you about life. Listen to the coach after the game while you are on a knee. If you do this from tee-ball through college baseball, you will have been presented the lessons to make you a strong, successful man. Now, it is up to you to put those life lessons and your knowledge to use in your upcoming years.

29. 5.6% of High School Seniors Will Play in College.

There were 130,100 senior high school baseball players last year. There were only 7,300 freshman college baseball players this year.

Do the math, even making a college baseball team is an accomplishment. If you have the ability and opportunity to play college baseball, do not pass it up. There are hundreds of thousands, possibly even millions of people who wish they could have played college baseball, but could not because of injury, health conditions, or simply lack baseball skills.

30. 10.5% of College Players Will Play Professional Baseball

This number seems somewhat appealing compared to the previous number. Wow! 10.5% of players will play professional baseball! Those are much better odds!

Not so fast. Professional baseball does not necessarily mean Major League Baseball. This stat relates to any form of professional baseball. There are some other professional baseball leagues besides the major and minor leagues. Any league in which the player has signed a contract to get paid to play for even one season counts as a professional baseball player, even if that player's salary is one dollar.

31. Just Because the Odds are Stacked Against You Doesn't Mean You Can't Make it!

Don't take this as me deterring you from your dream. This was once my dream too. Don't let anyone talk you out of going after your dreams. If every big leaguer thought they weren't going to make it, none of them would have made it. Just look at the numbers and take them for what they are worth. Anyone can do anything if they set their mind to it and take action.

32. Find Time to Call Loved Ones

Some might be thinking, what does this have to do with college baseball? Well, your family and friends back home may be the only people that will stand by you no matter what. Whether this season is your best or worst will not change the way these people view you and love you. Take the time to stay close with these people and let them know what they mean to you. Also, I said call, not text.

33. Stats aren't Everything

The public needs to be given this message as well. Many stats are skewed and don't tell the whole story. The college posts each player's batting average in a percentage. The college does not post or record how many times you have squared up a baseball and got out. The game is unfair at times and the stats don't mean everything. A pitcher can throw a no-hitter and get a loss next to his name based on errors, walks, hit batters, and dropped third strikes. Monitor the stats just for basic production purposes, but don't let them affect your performance or how you view others. After all, when your playing career is over, you will remember the great memories, moments, and stories more so than your stats.

34. People Look Up to You

Your siblings, hometown friends, old coaches, family members, and people you don't even know are watching your games, following your season and your team's season online. Don't let them down by doing something irresponsible. Make them proud. Do the right thing always and everywhere.

35. Expectations of a College Student

You are expected to go to class, learn what is required based on the curriculum and the teacher, and earn passing grades. Believe it or not poor academic performance can get you kicked off the team or you can lose your athletic eligibility.

36. Expectations of a College Athlete

When you are told something is mandatory, you must be there. When you are told something is optional, you should be there. You will gain respect of others by going to every single optional practice, workout, or session. You will lose respect by never going to anything optional. Be early to everything and stay late.

37. Umpires

NCAA umpires will not tolerate you expressing your opinions, displaying poor body language in their direction, or inappropriate language towards an opponent. Many high school umpires are hesitant to eject players or issue warning because they dread paperwork or filing reports. Collegiate umpires will not tolerate anything. If you disagree, keep it to yourself or wait until you get in the dugout to let out your frustration and even then, be cautious.

38. Haters and Doubters

Just as there are certain people who will always be on your side and rooting for you to succeed, there will also always be people who want you to fail. Now, these people may outwardly let you know they want you to fail or they may keep their opinions to themselves. The sad thing is many times your biggest haters can be roommates or people you consider to be friends. Sometimes these people are jealous of you, your status on campus, and/or your athletic ability in general. Be careful when choosing your college friends. Be sure these people will support you and truly care about you. There is someone out there hoping and thinking you're going to fail. Prove them wrong!

39. Professors

Your level of academic support depends on the professor. Some were athletes themselves and are more than understanding about missing class or required sessions for athletic practices or games. However, others can really give you a hard time about missing class and it will appear they are doing everything possible to make your life harder. On day one of each class, print and give your teacher your athletic schedule so there are no secrets or surprises as to where you will be on each day and why.

40. The Best Players aren't Always the Best People

A lot of people who dominate their craft become obsessed. To be the best you need to eat, sleep, and breathe baseball and nothing else. A tremendously accomplished basketball player, Kobe Bryant, admits to having put basketball before his family and friends while he was growing up. Sometimes people will look up to the best player on a team, until they meet that person in real life and spend enough time to develop a judgement on them. They might find out that that athlete is a great player, but is not a great person. Make sure you are able to differentiate the two when forming an opinion or judgement of someone.

41. Go to a Game

When deciding on a school and a baseball program it is key to go to a game and watch from first pitch to final out. Then, you must answer the following questions, "Can I play at this level?", "Will I play my freshman year?", "Am I okay being a bench player for 2 years then starting for 2 years or do I want to start all 4 years?"

42. The Mindset

At this level everyone has talent regardless of DI, DII, or DIII. Every player was "the man" in high school on their baseball team. Everyone was one of the best players at their high schools. What separates the good from the great at this level is the player's mindset. Are you mentally tough? Are you mature? Can you handle failure and not let it get you down? This game is hard enough to play against people, you cannot also be battling yourself and your own head. This is my best going against his best and may the best man win.

43. Eligibility

Your grades matter. Some programs have set higher standards for their students. To be NCAA eligible you must earn a 2.0 GPA or better, as well as be enrolled as a full-time student. If you are a part-time student you cannot compete in any athletic seasons in college per NCAA rules.

44. Transferring Rules

After you transfer, the following year you can compete in an athletic season. Each college has their own rules on how the college credits transfer over. All NCAA transfer rules are documented on a year by year basis on their website. These rules are always subject to change as the committee votes each year on a set of rules to make transferring colleges fair for the student and colleges involved.

45. Playing Multiple Sports

If you know someone in this day and age who was a two-sport athlete in college, God bless them. Playing one sport in college will drastically affect your college experience because of the amount of time, energy, and effort you must put forth on a daily basis to meet your expectations. Some coaches at some programs will make you pick one sport or the other because they know trying to do both is nearly impossible, but can be done within certain circumstances.

46. Meal Money

Each school has its own rules about meal money, but essentially the program is given a certain amount of money for food expenses for the team. Normally the team will either need to stop for a meal or the team will be provided a meal to save time on the way home. Be smart about how you use your money and it really becomes a skill analyzing any menu and trying to get the most bang for your buck.

47. Spring Break

Many colleges have a Spring Baseball Trip, in which the team goes to a different location to play baseball for a week against various teams. Many MLB fans would compare this to spring training, except the games count. This is the best week of the year because your only responsibility is baseball. It is spring break and unless you have schoolwork to get done, you can enjoy a week of playing the best game in the world with your some of best friends in nice weather.

48. Expect a Lot of Bunting

If you thought there was a lot of bunting in high school, wait until you get to college. Everyone can hit in college, but if you can hit and you can bunt, you present a serious offensive threat. Pitching is so dominant at the collegiate level that any chance the coach gets to move a runner over he will. If you want to give yourself serious value at the collegiate level, be able to sacrifice bunt consistently, as well as be able to consistently field a bunt.

49. Importance of Coaching

College baseball coaches often times stay in their locations for a very long time. The most successful programs always have the most successful coaches. Players come and go year by year and only have four years of eligibility, but head coaches can stay within a program as long as they would like if they keep winning. Coaching consistently successful teams at the collegiate level is a very difficult skill and these people are most responsible for building successful baseball programs.

50. More Games than the High School Season

At the DI level there is a maximum of 56 regular season games that can be played and at the DII and DIII level most teams play roughly a 30 to 40 game regular season. There are more games in a shorter period of time at this level. Thus, there is an increased importance of pitching and durable players.

51. Be Smart About Your Social Media

You are held to a higher standard as a student athlete. People follow your personal social media accounts and colleges have the power to see your accounts whether they are private or public. A general rule of thumb before posting anything anywhere is to read it over and if your mother wouldn't approve, don't click send. The college and your baseball program can punish any student who breaks their social media policies.

52. Conference Playoff Atmosphere

This is the collegiate version of a state or county tournament. If your team makes the playoffs in any level, you can expect to be holding your breath every pitch of every game. The atmosphere is unforgettable as teams compete to knock each other off in multiple playoff series that will determine the overall success of your season. After you have worked year round every day to become the best player you can be in order to help your team win their conference, you will understand the magnitude of these games.

53. Conference Pitchers

The conference games mean the most at the collegiate level. It does not matter if you are in a strong conference or a weak conference. Being named a conference game starting pitcher is an honor and should be the goal of every starting pitcher. Also, if you are a position player you want to be in the lineup for conference games no matter who the opponent is.

54. Lower Seams

The NCAA decided to lower the seams on their baseballs starting in 2015 in an attempt to boost offense. They found the pitchers were becoming too dominant and that lowering the seams would have a major impact on many pitchers' effectiveness. While you are in high school enjoy using those baseballs with the raised stitching atop the ball because once you get to college that ball changes. Many pitchers have lost the bite, break, and feel of a lot of their pitches from the high school to collegiate level.

55. The Baseball Gods

We all know baseball is a cruel sport in many ways. For example, you could lace a ball 380 feet into the gap that is caught by a diving outfielder or you could pull your head way off the ball and top a "swinging bunt" for a single in the books. In college, these same "gods" exist and the only way to succeed on this level is to have a positive outlook. In middle or high school you could probably get away with throwing your hands up in the air or intentionally displaying poor body language and sportsmanship. To experience sustained success in college, one must embrace the game even when it doesn't reward you for your effort and performance. You really need to just force positive energy into the mind and body for the best possible chance of successful performance. Again, this game is not for everyone and if you can't handle remarkably unlucky things happening to you or your team in the biggest of moments, you might want to find another sport.

56. Am I Sore or Am I Hurt?

This most commonly relates to arms, but can go for any body part. It is very important to be able to tell the difference between being sore and being hurt. Many players will have to learn to play through some soreness or discomfort because their team and teammates need and expect them to perform. However, if you are injured you are not expected to be on the field. You are expected to be doing everything in your power to heal your injury and get back on the field. Although this is not easy, it is a necessary skill if you want to get playing time. Constantly telling a coach or a trainer of something hurting will not get you on the field. No coach or trainer will ever put a player on the field if it means further injuring that individual, but a coach can and will expect you to give your best effort despite soreness. You know your body best and you ultimately must decide this - Am I sore or am I hurt?

57. Injuries

In athletics of all levels injuries can occur to any player at any time. In this case, it is always unfortunate and you never, ever root for anyone to get injured, but it's the next man up. The next person in line will be given a chance and they must make the most of their opportunity. Tom Brady's NFL career began the moment Drew Bledsoe got injured in Week 2 of the 2001 NFL season. He made the most of his opportunity to play and never looked back and there any many more examples of this throughout sports history. Injuries are very unfortunate and whether the player misses a game, a season, multiple seasons, or ends their career, someone must step up and fill that player's spot.

58. Teammates

Some teammates you might not be lifelong friends with and that is fine. But, there is something special about battling opponents with opponents 40+ times a year that bonds people together. Those teammates who fully buy into their team and their season are the most respected players on their teams. This game can bond people together for life. Undoubtedly, some of your teammates will be lifelong friends that you will visit and spend time with throughout the many years ahead. Your families and kids may even be friends and the friendship and bond will never die because of your time spent together on the baseball diamond.

59. Walk-up Songs

Whether you are a batter or a pitcher, most colleges play a brief part of a song while you are warming up on the mound or walking to the plate. On some teams, the older players get to choose the freshmen's walk-up songs. This can be quite humorous as the walk-up song is meant to energize and pump-up the player and the crowd, yet artists like Taylor Swift or Britney Spears tend to play a different style of music than what is expected in an athletic setting.

60. Body Language

Body language can make or break you as a college baseball player. A random spectator should be able to come to the game at any point and not be able to realize who is winning or losing without looking at the scoreboard. All players on the field are expected to be "locked in" to the game and maintain positive energy and effort regardless of outstanding or poor performance. Every single college coach will talk to the team at one point or another about body language throughout a season, so clearly, this is very important.

61. The Bullpen

Every coach has different expectations for relief pitchers but these players undoubtedly are some of the funniest players on the team. They have the important responsibility of "putting out the fire." They must come into a close game or a blow out and get outs for their team. Yet, because these players have so much down time, many learn how to keep things light and fun until called upon to perform. If the coach requires all players to stay in the dugout, relievers must be more serious and focused. However, if your coach allows relief pitchers to sit in the bullpen, expect to hear some funny stories or see some bullpen shenanigans occurring throughout the course of a college baseball game.

62. Down Time

There are a lot of times before and after practice or games that baseball players need to entertain themselves with competitive games to make the time pass. For example, some classic games include pepper, 2-ball, and stopwatch baseball. These games are also effective during rain delays or bus rides.

63. Fungo Golf

Arguably the greatest "free time" activity in all of college baseball. You can play 9 or 18 holes. The game starts with a player choosing the location for the next hole - such as "The 325 sign in Right-Center." Each player will then "tee-off" and using a baseball and fungo bat drive their ball as close to the hole as possible. Each player uses their own ball and strikes the ball off a self-toss. Each contact with the bat counts as a stroke, as well as a swing and miss. The ball must hit the exact spot chosen as the hole for the hole to be completed. The winner of each hole then decides the location for the next hole. Different rules are used based on who you are playing with, but I encourage you to play a round with your teammates, as it will enhance your college baseball experience.

64. Pitch Counts

Pitch counts play a bigger role in today's game more so than any other baseball era. As a batter, you will learn the importance of taking pitches and driving up a pitcher's pitch count. Conversely, pitchers' approaches are more aggressive than ever knowing that starters will likely not go much further than 100 pitches. Therefore, pitchers need to fill the zone with as many strikes as possible as early as possible, rather than "nibbling" around the plate early in the at bat. As a hitter, the first strike you see will likely be the best pitch you are going to get to hit the entire at bat. If you are a batter who fouls a lot of pitches off and sees a lot of pitches from the opponent, you will find yourself in the line-up much more often than the "free swinger" who swings at everything.

100 is merely an arbitrary number that is used by many coaches at the collegiate and MLB level. Although every coach seems to have their own opinion on pitch counts, the coach's theory that makes the most sense to me is Bobby Valentine. Valentine's theory is that being at 100 pitches in 4 innings is much different than 100 pitches in 8 innings and coaches need to get away from the magic 100 pitches and you are out. If you have thrown 100 pitches in 4 innings, you have had deep counts, guys on base, and runs scored against you. You may have thrown these 100 pitches within an hour if your team keeps having quick half innings up at the plate. Throwing that many pitches in that short of a time fatigues your arm and body much more than throwing 100 pitches through 8 innings with a lot of rest in between innings because your team keeps scoring. This makes the most sense as you think about the human body. The 4 inning example equates to 25 pitches an inning. The 8 inning example equates to 12.5 pitches an inning. Clearly the difference is huge. Knowing and understanding this concept can help both the offensive and defensive players choose their approach to the game.

65. Dipping

If you haven't encountered this in your baseball career yet, I can guarantee you will in college baseball. Now, chewing tobacco is prohibited at all levels of baseball, including the MLB. As of 2016, Major League Baseball began prohibiting the use of all forms of chewing or smokeless tobacco at major league stadiums. Chewing tobacco, or "dip", as it is commonly referred to, has been linked to baseball for so many years. Some of your teammates will likely chew tobacco. So, be prepared for someone to offer you dip throughout your college baseball career. It is important to avoid all forms of tobacco to maintain healthy gums and teeth.

66. Your Reputation

You only have one name in this life. You want others to have nothing but good things to say about you as a person and also about you as a player. Your reputation will determine how much respect you are given by your teammates, coaches, and the opponent. Do the right thing on and off the field.

67. Profanity

Sometimes athletes of all ages and of all sports express their frustration through the use of profanity. Now I am not going to tell you that using swear words is acceptable, but if it is going to happen, make it very rarely and under your breath. Cursing out loud after walking a batter, striking out, or missing a ball will likely land you on the bench at this level. Additionally, one of the umpires will likely have a conversation with you or issue you a warning. This game is hard enough to play as it is without all the negative self-talk and poor body language. Find a different way to release your frustration and anger that will help prepare you for your next opportunity.

68. Off-season Rules

In college baseball, teams of all divisions have a fall season in which teams can formally run organized practices, scrimmages, and games. However, in the summer and the winter, baseball teams may not meet with their college coaches and formally practice, workout, or play. Teammates can work out, hit, throw, etc. with one another but doing so with any more than 4 players and using team issued equipment/facilities is considered an illegal practice session if a coach is present. Thus, many teams call "captain's practices." At these informal practices, players can get and stay in shape without violating any NCAA rules.

69. High School Stats

Don't be the player who brags about your high school ERA or batting average. You will learn that everyone in college baseball was a great high school player and what you did in the past doesn't really matter. Be humble and prove how good of a player you are now and at this level.

70. Freshman Pranks

This will happen to you and if it does not happen to you it will happen to one of your teammates. Examples of this will not be shared so as not to spoil one of the many memories you will never forget. Instead of stressing or worrying about the one time all year someone might play a prank on you, just laugh and enjoy the moment with your teammates.

71. Rain Delays and Rainouts

"Sometimes you win, sometimes you lose, sometimes it rains."
- Bull Durham (1988).

You can't control the weather so instead of worrying about it and stressing over it, simply prepare like you normally would. Sometimes rainouts and rain delays lead to the funniest and best memories of an entire season. You might be in a gym playing wiffle ball with the whole team or having a dance off against the opponent in the rain.

72. Signs

Knowing the signs won't get you on the field, but *not* knowing the signs sure will get you off the field. If you put the time and energy into memorizing the signs your freshman year this will come naturally and require no additional "study time" for the rest of your college career. Nothing frustrates a coach more than a player who misses or does not know the signs, so study them with your roommates, teammates, or whoever. Just do yourself a favor and make sure you know them!

73. Plays

Along with knowing the signs it is crucial to know all of the defensive plays. Some coaches use obscure visual or verbal methods to relay signs or shifts to the defense regarding 1st and 3rd's, pick-offs, and bunt defenses.

74. Seeds and Gum

Another reason baseball is so great is because it is one of the only sports in which you can eat while playing. Especially in college, many players chew seeds or gum while up at the plate, in the field, or in the dugout. Some do it because science proves chewing gum increases focus and concentration. Others do it because they are hungry or just want to. You need to find what works for you. Maybe those things distract you and are not for you during gameplay.

75. White Cleats and White Batting Gloves

There is a certain stigma surrounding players who wear white cleats or have white batting gloves. That stigma is not a positive one. You better be batting .400 or better or be the best pitcher in the conference to do these things. There's no real reason behind it, but white cleats and white batting gloves gets people's attention, in a negative way.

76. Three-quarter Sleeve Shirts

If you are a pitcher, load up on these. Some coaches require it and some don't but covering your elbow as a pitcher has always been important for health and success. Your body always performs better when you are warm than if you are cold, regardless of position or sport. That is the main reason why all teams at all levels "warm up." It is proven to increase performance and decrease the potential for injury.

77. Look like a Ball Player

Tuck your jersey in and wear your hat forward. Wear your pants up or wear your pants down, none of this one sock stuff. This game has been doing just fine for hundreds of years and is a game that requires class and professionalism at all levels. Also, nobody wants to see your obscure, personal fashion statements.

78. Have No Regrets

Go do it. The biggest regrets people have are the things they decided not to do. So whatever you are unsure of, just go for it. If you don't fully commit to baseball, a few years down the road you may regret it because that opportunity has passed. If a senior player invites you to workout with him, go for it. Why not? Have no regrets.

79. Contribute in Any Way You Can

If you are not in the starting line-up, do not sulk and slump at the end of the bench for 9 innings. First of all, you are being selfish and only worried about your playing time and not the success of the team. Secondly, the coach will certainly not sub you into the game. When you display poor body language and a disheartened attitude, you will not be called upon in the 8th inning to lay a bunt down, pinch run, pinch hit, or be a defensive replacement.

Find a way to contribute to the team's success. You can fill out charts, keep the scorebook, retrieve foul balls, keep the pitch count, organize the helmets and the bats after each inning, warm up the left-fielder, or just bring an enormous amount of energy and life to the dugout. Some bench players steal the opponents' batting or pitching signs. Some bench players stare at the pitcher until they notice something that is tipping off the pitch they are going to throw. "Coach, every time this guy throws his changeup he wipes his pants after getting the sign." You can have an impact on the game without physically playing in the game. Your coaches and teammates will notice and appreciate your effort and support.

80. Sunglasses

There are a few big baseball brand sunglasses such as Oakley, Nike, and Under Armour but the brand does not matter. Just invest in a nice pair of sunglasses that have a case. Over the course of playing and training outdoors for 4 years in the spring, summer, and fall it will be worth the investment. The cheap 10 dollar sunglasses will break in your bag or on the bench and you'll continuously be buying new ones.

81. Fundraising

Expect to be asked to fundraise. Every program has different fundraising strategies, but give full effort because the money either goes to the team or the athletic department and that money, in turn, eventually comes back to you in possible forms such as new uniforms, bats, socks, etc.

82. Take a Sports Psychology Class

If sport psychology is offered at your college, find a way to take the class within the time you are at the institution. Many athletes have sworn their performance has never increased more than after they have completed a sports psychology course. This class might be just what you need and are missing to really push you over the edge from good to great or role player to starter. Training the mind is just as valuable, if not more valuable as training the body as it relates to baseball performance.

83. Weighted Balls

Some schools utilize a weighted ball program in an attempt to keep player's arms healthy, as well as increase velocity. My advice would be to keep an open mind to it. Many players really believe in the theory and science behind it, some don't know the science behind it and do it anyway, and some just want nothing to do with it. Sometimes by simply changing your mindset and buying into a training principle it can prove to be beneficial. For example, if your mind is telling you the entire time no matter what it is you are doing, "Don't get hurt," many times you end up getting hurt. However, if you are fully invested and convinced this is going to work and make me better, many times it does.

84. Ask the Coach How You Can Improve

Don't be afraid to ask the head coach or any assistant coach what you can do to improve. Now, asking him why he is not playing you or why he decided to make a certain move may be more of a touchy subject as these decisions are his call and his job, but never be afraid to ask how you can improve. The coach wants you to improve and will be honest with you. No coach will ever say to any athlete, "Johnny, there is nothing you can possibly improve on. You are perfect in every possible way."

So, your goal should be to get a few specific things you can do to get better that will increase your value and help the team win. For instance, a coach might respond saying, "You need to increase your speed because next year we will be losing our top 3 base stealers and we need a guy with base stealing capability." Or he might talk more about your current performances, "You just need to get back to the basics of hitting. Your fundamentals seemed off and you appeared discouraged at the plate. For you to help this team win, we need you to be able to bat for average." Plus, the coach will like that you are driven and want to improve, no matter how good you already are.

85. The Truth about Sports Drinks

Many MLB dugouts have Gatorade coolers inside them, but rarely are they actually filled with Gatorade. This is because the sports drinks really aren't good for the body. In fact, Gatorade is a lot like soda. The main ingredients in a bottle of Gatorade are water, sucrose syrup, glucose-fructose syrup, citric acid, natural flavors, salt, sodium citrate, and monopotassium phosphate. The main ingredients in a bottle of Pepsi are carbonated water, high fructose corn syrup, caramel color, sugar, phosphoric acid, caffeine, citric acid, and natural flavors. The two are eerily similar. Now if you are someone who drinks sports drinks simply for the taste I understand that. If you are someone who drinks sports drinks to increase hydration, recovery, and performance, you need to do a little more research as to what exactly you are putting in your body. Rather than reaching for a sports drink, stick to water or try coconut water for your hydration and recovery needs.

86. Get a Lacrosse Ball and a Foam Roller

These two aid in improving recovery and flexibility. I recommend every baseball player get one of each and use them to relieve sore and overworked muscles regardless of the position you play. Performance has been proven to increase by relieving the sore, tender, and tight muscles within the body.

87. Look Good, Feel Good, Play Good

This is a real phenomenon in which one's performance in destined to improve if they like the way they look. However, the only opinion that matters is one's own opinion. If you like the way you look you are more probable to have a better opinion of one's self, experience more self-confidence, and therefore perform better. Some players don't wear sleeves or batting gloves because they like the way it makes them look. Other players like to tape their wrists, wear elbow and shin guards when batting, and sport the latest and greatest pair of batting gloves. Doing or not doing these things does not make you a better or worse baseball player, but not liking how you look can make you a worse performer.

88. Use Your Warm ups

This goes for all aspects of the game of baseball. In college baseball, you are expected to make the most of every opportunity and be as prepared as possible for those opportunities. This means that in between innings, if you are an infielder, come get a good hop and deliver a strike to first with the same mechanics, effort, and speed you plan to use if a ball is hit to you during the inning. If you are the on-deck batter you are timing up the pitcher and focusing on small cues that are going to help you be successful. If you are the pitcher you will be given 8 warm up pitches the first inning you enter the game. Every inning after that you will be given 5 warm up pitches. Use these pitches effectively throughout the game to help you spot and command all of your pitches once the batter steps in and the inning starts for real. Players that waste time, use bad mechanics, and don't try during their opportunities to warm up are less successful than those who are well prepared.

89. I/O

Infield/outfield is practiced many times in practice so that when you take I/O before the game everyone is on the same page. Because everyone comes from a different high school, it is important to learn this in the pre-season so everyone knows what the team is doing and also why the team is doing it. When the opponent takes I/O is your chance to watch and scout the opponent's players in the field.

90. Come off The Bus Dressed

A scout once told me that they lost interest in a player because they did not like the way the player got off the bus. He wore flip flops, an untucked jersey, a sideways hat, and those really big headphones. The scout crossed him off the list and left without ever seeing the kid play. Now some might say that is awfully judgmental, but the scout explained to me that his program is looking for players who are anxious and eager every time they get to the ballpark. This player was laid back, lackadaisical, and not prepared to start warming up. Get off the bus with your jersey tucked in, pants on, hat on, and either turf shoes or cleats on. This way when you walk to the dugout you can drop your bag and head out to the outfield for warm ups. The whole team won't have to wait for you to get situated to warm up. It is an unnecessary waste of time.

91. Physical Errors are Acceptable, Mental Errors are not

If you are as prepared for the opportunity as possible, know the situation, and know your job, but you do not execute most coaches won't be mad at you. However, if you are missing any part of that formula, the coach has a very good reason to be upset.

There is no reason you shouldn't be prepared. There is no reason why you shouldn't know the situation. And there is no reason you should not know your job. Physicals errors are going to happen, mental errors cannot. You need to know how many outs there are at this level … you just need to. You need to know the signs. You need to know the score and where the other runners are.

92. KISS

This principle can be used at all levels of baseball. KISS is an acronym for Keep, It, Simple, Stupid. College baseball can tear your mind apart if you overthink every situation and every play. Keep it simple. Know your job and do your job. There is no use in spending time and energy thinking about the past because the past is the past. It's over and done with. Just focus on your next opportunity to do something great, which is this next pitch.

93. Steroids

This is not as common at the college level as in higher levels, but the NCAA does test for anabolic agents. The NCAA spends roughly $6 million annually on drug testing of all kinds. There are so many other ways and techniques to improve your performance than to get involved in HGH or any kind of anabolic steroid use. Just stay away.

94. Sending a Message

Again, this is not as common at the NCAA level as it is at higher levels, but baseball is baseball. There may be a time in which you or someone on your team feels they have intentionally been hit by a pitch or your pitcher may have hit an opponent intentionally. This can lead to bad blood between teams and possibly even bench-clearing activity. However, this is normally not done out of nowhere. Either the pitcher or the team may feel the need to "send a message" to the opponent that they will not tolerate certain things. For example, many teams will not accept someone running the score up on them, sliding with their spikes up with intention to hurt players, or taunting and overly celebrating on the field.

95. Gambling Rules

No college athlete is allowed to formally gamble in anyway. It is technically an NCAA violation to play fantasy sports, fill out March madness brackets, or even play poker with the team for money.

96. Hazing, Bullying, and Harassment

These are serious policies that the colleges themselves and the NCAA will not tolerate or accept. There are consequences both at the NCAA and individual college level for these acts whether they happen on or off the field.

97. Size Doesn't Matter

Well, size kind of doesn't matter. For example, a taller pitcher does, in fact, release the ball closer to the plate than a shorter pitcher. However, size is not the only factor and is not looked at as the determining factor to a player's value. There are many different body types within the sport and not all of the most successful college baseball players are the biggest or strongest.

98. Pitching Rotations & Roles

The pitching roles within a college team are as follows: conference starting pitcher, non-conference starting pitcher, relief pitcher, and closer. Many times people will argue the starting pitcher is the key factor in determining the outcome of the game. It does not matter how dominant the starter is if he goes 7 shutout inning and the bullpens blows the game in the final two. The importance of a strong bullpen is now changing the way MLB and college teams assemble their pitching staff each year. All of these pitching roles are different, but they are all important. You may have been a starting pitcher your entire life and be asked your freshman season to come in from the bullpen and that is okay. You will learn the differences and how to succeed with time, effort, and dedication to a new role and new craft.

99. Team Traditions & Routines

Every team has different traditions and routines they embrace throughout the course of a season. Some of them are formally and publicly done, while others are more informal and only involve team members. It is important to learn your freshman year about these traditions and their significance.

100. Assistant Coaches

Sometimes you will learn more from the assistants than you do the head coach. Many times the head coach trusts the assistants to run practice or individual, position-based drills. The head coach is responsible for the program as a whole. He is responsible for making all the playing decisions, in game decisions, and all things relating to the formality of the team, such as overall record and scheduling games. You must learn to embrace the assistant coaches and pick up as much information you can from each of them.

101. You Never Know Who's Watching

It's true. An MLB scout could be in attendance at the game. He could be coming to see you, specifically. He could be at the game to watch a teammate of yours or an opponent. He could be at the game watching his nephew, friend's son or his own son play. Who knows? The exciting unknown of baseball is that you never know who is watching. This means you must represent yourself and your team to the best of your ability in all things that you do both on and off the field. If you keep this in mind every time you play a game, I can guarantee you will act and behave differently in the field, at the plate, in the dugout, on the bases, or even chasing foul balls.

102. All Sisters are Off Limits

This could be the best lesson you will learn in this entire book. This goes for all teammates and all close friends before, during, and after college. Of course you can be friendly and nice to your friends' sisters, but definitely do not pursue anything further if you really care about your buddy. Just to be clear, <u>all</u> sisters are off limits.

103. Plagiarism

Do your own work, it's not worth it to copy. If you submit plagiarized work in college and get caught you can fail the assignment, fail the class, or even be expelled from the institution. It just isn't worth it and tutors and extra credit are offered and readily available at almost all colleges. Your academic advisor and professor can help find and schedule academic help for you.

104. The Game Within the Game

The lessons you learn in college baseball will roll over into your life. In both baseball and in life you must be as prepared as you possibly can be and give as much effort as you have. Now, although doing this does not guarantee you success, your probability of being successful increases dramatically in both baseball and life when you are prepared and giving maximum effort. Assuming you have failed at least once in baseball or in life before, how do you respond?

What is your response to failure? Do you blame others or hold yourself accountable? So what if that 1-1 curveball was a little outside. No one cares that it started raining during your at bat. No one cares that the ball hit a pebble as it came to you and skipped over your glove. Your coaches and teammates at the collegiate level will not put up with excuses. Make plays, not excuses.

As this carries over into your life outside of baseball or life after baseball, you are expected to get the job done. You will be accountable to your boss, your colleagues, and your family and none of those people want to hear your excuses either. Your boss won't care that your dog kept you up all night and that's why you are late. Your colleagues have a lot going on at home too and are getting their jobs done well and on time. Your kids won't want to hear how busy you are with your work; they want you at their tee ball games. Stop making excuses and get the job done!

105. Roommates

At some colleges you have the option to choose your roommate freshman year and at other colleges you are assigned a random roommate. Find a way to get through your freshman year and then you can select a roommate or roommates to live with from sophomore year on. However, it is vital that you make a wise selection for a roommate. You will start to become very similar to the people you choose to surround yourself with. I would suggest choosing a player on the baseball team that you are close friends with, but also that you hold similar values and beliefs as. This is not meant in the religious sense, but in the sense of your priorities. For example, is getting enough sleep important to both of you? Is getting good grades important to both of you? Is working out or getting extra repetitions before or after practice important to you? Choosing a roommate is a huge decision and I would suggest taking the time to weigh your options and consider the different lifestyle each person lives before choosing a roommate.

106. Gloves

Your knowledge of gloves will grow exponentially playing baseball in college. To this point you might just know some popular brands and which positions wear larger or smaller sizes. I would recommend buying an expensive glove that will last your entire college career, but I would not do this until spring of your freshman year, just in case the coaches want to try you in a new position, you did not just waste a lot of money. Some popular, well-known baseball brands for gloves are Rawlings, Wilson, Mizuno, Louisville Slugger, Easton, Marcucci, Evoshield, and Franklin Sports.

It is important that you take care of your nice glove. The way baseball gloves get ruined is by sitting in baseball bags. When you are transporting your glove from place to place or it is not being used for months during the winter it cannot sit crunched up in a baseball bag. To keep your glove in good condition over a long period of time it must simply be carried or clipped onto the bag. Think about it. You play a game in the rain and your cleats get muddy. Then you put your cleats and glove in the same bag. Then you throw your bag under the bus for the ride home and your bag is now underneath everyone else's bag and the team gear and then you wonder the next day why your glove looks the way it does.

Finally, don't go sticking your hand in anyone's glove without asking first. Some people are extremely particular and superstitious about their gloves like you would not believe. Others, however, do not care.

107. Parents

At the collegiate level, the parent's role in their child's success is smaller than it once was in youth leagues and high school baseball. Parents should not feel neglected or shy in terms of their interactions with their son, his teammates, and the coaches whatsoever. However, it is important that your parents are smart in terms of time and place. Before, after, or in between games is not the time for your parents to come in the dugout or ask the coaches questions. The parents take a back seat in their son's dreams at this stage in their life. It is now that the ball player decides how serious he is about baseball moving forward and what baseball means to him, while away from his family and hometown. Parents still play an enormous role in supporting their son in any way that they can, but there is less physical parent and baseball contact than there probably once was.

108. The Intangibles

These are the qualities that make-up a baseball player that are not measured with statistical value or easily seen on paper such as height, weight, batting average, etc. These are qualities that coaches at all levels look for players to possess, regardless of the level: work ethic, love of the game, "heart", serious competitor, and good character. If you are someone who possesses these intangibles you bring tremendous value to your team and are also setting yourself up to live a successful life outside of the game.

109. The Outside Pitch

This is the safe pitch. Knowing what the pitchers at this level are trying to do will help make you a better hitter. The outside pitch might as well be called the safe pitch because it is very rare that a pitch away can seriously hurt you, as a pitcher. At the high school level, a varsity pitcher will throw anywhere between 80 and 90% away fastballs. Think about it, if the pitcher misses his spot too far away, it is merely a ball. If the pitcher paints the black with a fastball on the corner one of three things will happen. First, the batter could take the pitch and he will have earned himself a strike. Second, the batter could try to pull the away pitch and will either swing and miss or will roll over and hit a weak ground ball. Finally, the batter could see the ball deep and hit it where it is pitched, serving the ball the opposite way for a single. It is rare that the batter will drive the ball the other way over the outfielder's head, but it does happen. The difference between a good hitter and a great one is can the batter go the other way. To be successful at the college level and beyond, the hitter must be able to hit the away pitch. Almost everyone can hit the inside pitch. It is not nearly as difficult to hit the inside pitch. After all is said and done, the pitcher could also miss the away spot to the inside and leave the ball over the plate, which at this level will result in one of two things. The pitch right down the middle will be hammered, or the batter will swing and just miss it or miss entirely. The outside pitch is the safe pitch for pitchers.

110. The Inside Pitch

Again understanding this concept is just as valuable for hitters to know exactly how the pitchers are trying to get you out. Now the inside pitch is a game changer in college. Pitchers who are not confident in their velocity or movement are very reluctant to pitch anyone inside because it is much easier for a batter to turn on a flat fastball on the inside of the plate. Additionally, the inside pitch is a much more dangerous pitch for the pitcher to make because if he misses too far inside, he could hit the batter. If he hits his spot on the inside corner he will either get the strike call or the batter will swing. Lastly, if the pitcher misses his inside spot, the ball is right down the pipe and will likely be smoked. So if you think about it, the outside pitch has much less of a chance of a negative result for the pitcher. Thus, this is why many high school pitchers exclusively hit only outside spots. Once you get to college you need to be able to pitch inside. It is crucial. The inside pitch is very effective if you can simply hit your spots and it does not allow the hitter to "sit" on the away pitch and flare the ball the opposite way. At this level the batters were all the best batters at their high schools and can hit the away pitch with regularity the other way. Undoubtedly, if the pitcher has the accuracy, control, and confidence to pitch inside as well as outside, he will experience much more success. Similarly, the hitter that can turn on the inside pitch, as well as go with the outside pitch will also experience much success.

111. Collegebaseballcamps.com

If you have not yet decided what college to attend, this is a great resource for you to explore. Colleges and universities post their prices, dates, and details for interested student athletes to attend a camp on their campus. Players have the opportunities to perform on the college's field in front of the college's coaches. This experience is proven to help players and their families learn more about the college and the baseball program, as well as gives the coaches a chance to evaluate potential prospects.

112. Sport Specific Training

Previously we addressed the team lifts and different weight lifting and training sessions some programs use. The best advice I can give you to be healthy and successful is to be sure you are being sport specific when you work out. Yes lifting weights is valuable, but extremely heavy lifts in season is definitely not recommended. It is very tempting as a young man in college to become a "gym rat" and want to get as big as possible.

Baseball players should train like baseball players and power-lifters should train like powerlifters. Training like a baseball player means doing things that your position requires. Baseball players should be throwing, running, fielding, and hitting. Gym time should be dedicated to areas of the body that will not interfere or hinder one's ability to play the game or be healthy. The counter argument to this perspective is that many MLB players are extremely strong and lift heavy weights all the time. This is true, but many MLB players are also beginning to rethink their training strategies due to injury. Baseball players these days are bigger, faster, and stronger than ever before. However, these players are also getting injured more frequently than ever before. The nature of the game does not require one to have a body-builder's body. The game requires flexibility, speed, arm strength, bat speed, baseball intelligence, and extreme focus over a long period of time. So, this begs one to question, "Why train like a bodybuilder if you play baseball?" To ensure your longevity and increase your skills that are transferable to the actual game, train like a baseball player, after all, that is what you are.

113. Pre-Game Meal

Whether away or home it is important that you time up your pre-game meal and fuel your body with nutrients that will help you perform at your best. It does not matter how good you are, your performance will decrease if you head to the field right after eating a burrito and chocolate milk. You want to eat carbohydrates before your athletic events, preferably simple carbohydrates. These foods are easily digestible and your body can easily transfer the food into energy. Meanwhile, fats and proteins are much harder for the human body to process and thus take longer to transfer into energy. Additionally, if you eat a large meal before the game you can easily become tired because your body must work extremely hard to process and digest the massive amounts of food you just consumed. An example of a good pre-game meal would be toast with jelly, a banana, and a bottle of water.

114. Girlfriends

Depending on your major and the level of baseball you are competing at, having a girlfriend can be very difficult. The name of the game in college is time management. Do not be surprised if while "in-season" you have little to no free time for dates, as you are expected to be a student-athlete and that is not easy to do these days.

115. Height and Handedness

As previously mentioned height does not matter in the sense that there are positions for those of all different body types. In general, coaches want a taller first basemen that can scoop very well because this helps the infielder make their throws. A tall first baseman provides are huge target for the infield to throw to. On the other hand, there are very rarely tall catchers. Catching is not an easy position for taller players based on the wear and tear done to your knees and hips as the player spends the majority of his time in the crouched position. Now, most of you are aware of these facts by now. The point is that height and handedness cannot be learned, taught, or easily altered. There is no other sport in which lefties are more valuable to have on a team than baseball. Many times a lefty pitcher throwing 80 to 90 miles per hour can make a Division I baseball team. However, if you are a right handed pitcher, it is very difficult to crack a Division I roster without throwing 90+. If you have tall height or are a lefty the D-I coaches believe they can teach you how to better utilize your body and mechanics to throw harder. But you can't choose or change your height or handedness. The moral of the story is as much as the intangibles can get you on a collegiate baseball team, your height and handedness often play a large role in your position and status on the depth chart on your specific team.

116. Your Number

You may have been a specific number your whole life, but in college that will likely change. It is so rare that you will get your number that it really should not be thought about. Sure it is a good feeling playing the game you love with your favorite number on, but your focus should really be on making the team and working your way into the starting line-up. Most of the time, jersey numbers are based on seniority so while your number might be taken while you are an underclassman, it could open up by junior or senior year.

117. Walks

There is nothing that frustrates a coach as much as pitchers walking batters. The quickest way to get in the doghouse with your coach is to struggle to throw strikes. Coaches would much rather see your pitches get hit and hit hard than for you to throw balls. At least if the ball is hit there are fielders positioned out there with a chance to make a play to get the team an out. When you walk the opponent you do not give your team a chance to make an out. If you are a position player and batter, coaches love players with a good eye. This does not mean try to draw a walk every at bat, but the coach cannot ask anything more of you than to swing at strikes and take balls. This is a tough skill to acquire and is only developed with many repetitions.

118. Intrinsic Motivation

Most college athletes are intrinsically motivated, meaning they are passionate and driven by themselves and from within. People who are extrinsically motivated are driven by outside awards or rewards. For examples, these are the guys who play sports for the girls, parties, popularity, or social status and not a genuine and true love of the game. They don't love hard work or the grind, but they do love the perks that come along with being a college baseball player. Intrinsically motivated athletes work hard when no one's watching. These people are in it for the love of the game and because they genuinely want to be there. This is the type of athlete you should strive to be. Many coaches argue that this self-driven philosophy cannot be taught or learned and that athletes either possess it or they don't.

119. Learning How to Lose

The common phrase in athletics is, "You need to learn how to lose before you can learn how to win." This mantra directly relates to baseball, but does not promote losing. Within any given day you can experience failure, but it is how you handle that failure that will determine how successful you will be. There are some players that get out in their first at bat and they carry their negative emotion into the field with them and into their next at bat. These players have not learned how to "lose" yet. They are not good at moving on and leaving the past in the past. In baseball you must learn how to handle and overcome failure. The common misconception of this phrase is that only coaches of losing teams promote this phrase, which is not true. The message is that if you cannot overcome "losing" you will never win.

120. Dietary Supplements

You are going to want to check that all of your supplements are allowed with your athletic department staff, if you choose to take supplements. Some supplements can cause a positive drug test even though they may only be a vitamin or mineral. Supplements are not well regulated. While most food and drink products are formally regulated by the FDA, no supplements are required to be regulated by any governing body. Therefore, all supplements you choose to take you do so at your own risk. Some supplements contain NCAA banned substances that are not presented on the label.

121. NCAA Banned Substances

Before the season begins, players are required to sign a compliance form agreeing to follow all NCAA rules and regulations. The NCAA has the right to randomly drug test players on any program and if any of the below substances are detected the player will serve a suspension and miss game or even could lose eligibility. If a player refuses to take a drug test, they are assumed to be "guilty" and will serve a suspension or lose eligibility. The NCAA classifies their banned substances into 8 categories: stimulants, anabolic agents, alcohol and beta blockers, diuretics and other masking agents, street drugs, peptide hormones and analogues, anti-estrogens, and beta-2 agonists.

122. Restricted Procedures and Drugs

The NCAA does not allow blood doping, gene doping, local anesthetics, manipulation of urine samples, or beta-2 agonists. Drug tests may not be cheated or manipulated and if a player is caught, they are assumed "guilty" and are recorded as failing a drug test and will face a suspension or loss of eligibility.

123. MLB Draft

Players at a four-year college or university become eligible for the Major League Baseball draft upon completion of their third year or after their 21st birthday, whichever comes first. Players from junior colleges or community colleges are eligible for the MLB draft at any time.

Players can also become eligible for the Rule 4 draft:

- If they have graduated from high school
- Their high school athletic eligibility has expired
- They dropped out of high school at least 365 days prior to the draft
- They have attended a junior college the previous year
- Are attending a four-year college and have completed at least junior year of eligibility
- Are attending a four-year college and is 21 or older
- Are attending a four-year college that does not have a baseball program
- Were dismissed from a four-year college for academic reasons
- Withdrew from a four-year college at least 120 days prior to the draft.

124. Yoga

Believe it or not many college baseball players use yoga as a way to recover during the baseball season. Yoga is proven to increase flexibility, muscle strength, muscle tone, energy, vitality, athletic performance. Additionally, yoga decreases stress and the risk of injury. Although this practice is not for everyone, many players end up utilizing yoga as a part of their in season training for the reasons listed above.

125. Arm Injuries

With the increase volume of baseball activity from high school to college, many players experience their first arm injury their freshman year of college. These injuries can happen at all different times throughout one's baseball career, but some will never have an arm injury. Throwing a baseball is not a natural motion. The human body was not designed to throw a 5 ounce baseball overhand at high speeds on a daily basis. To have a successful and fulfilling baseball career, you must be on the field and not hurt. Although these injuries cannot fully be prevented, the risk of injuring yourself drastically decreases when you warm up before your throw or practice. Many coaches utilize the phrase, "You warm up to throw. You do not throw to warm up." By breaking a sweat and activating the different muscles throughout your entire body before any physical activity, you are preparing your muscles for use and are more likely to remain healthy.

126. Who Exactly are the Coaches?

Who are they? Well, this can be different for every program

based on the athletic department. Sometimes the head coach is just a head baseball coach for the college. Other times, the head baseball coach may also be a professor at the college. You might have a coach who is a paid assistant that gets a stipend for his coaching duties and time and whether they work another job or not is up to them. Anyone who is a volunteer coach is volunteering their time to your team without getting paid. Finally, one or more of your coaches could be a graduate assistant. Graduate assistant coaches are pursuing their graduate degree at the college and are getting a portion of or their entire tuition paid for in return of their coaching services. Any collegiate baseball coach deserves your respect and you need to listen and learn from them. Some of you may want to be a graduate assistant coach after your college baseball career is over and you want to pursue a coaching career, as well as earn a graduate degree.

127. Superstition

All baseball players are superstitious to a certain degree. Now some college players and teams are more superstitious than others. For instance, in the 2017 College Baseball World Series the Florida Gators rallied behind a paper cup that had fallen over the dugout railing and onto the field.. Yes, a cup. In that same half-inning the Gators took the lead over the LSU Tigers and refused to pick the cup back up, even when coaches tried to pick it up off the field. The team guarded that cup because it brought them good luck and moving it could prove to be risky.

Now this is just one example of hundreds and thousands of superstitions that have developed for different players and teams over the years, but some are more serious than others. These players seriously relied on that cup staying there and would not let anyone touch it or move it. Some baseball players think it is bad luck to let other people put their hands in their glove. Some pitchers go to the back of the mound and write a meaningful word or symbol in the dirt behind the rubber. The matter of fact is that superstition will always be a part of baseball and learning what your college team's superstitious beliefs are will save you from learning the hard way and catching flack during the season.

128. Brawls

It is very rare for a college game to ever lead to a brawl. If a player or a team have a problem with how an opponent is acting, they usually let him know it right away. For example, if a player were to hit a homerun and drastically showboat around the bases, the position players have a duty to "jaw" at him as he goes around the bases. The bench and the catcher are also expected to let him know that is not acceptable. No team wants their opponent to disrespect or embarrass them. The biggest difference between what you see in an MLB game and a college game is that the opponent will not wait to plunk you with a pitch. The other team will get right in your face and let you know that you are not going to do that against us. In the majors, many times you will see the other team let the player have their moment and then 3 innings later hit him with a pitch to send a message. Play the game the right way and these situations are avoided.

129. Fields

All fields are different obviously, but this plays a large role in the college game. The different dimensions can alter how pitchers attacks hitters. Some fields may have a short porch in right field or left field and some may have extremely large dimensions. At this level every inch counts and can change the outcome of a game. Part of the reason coaches get their teams to the field so early is so they can get used to the surface. Is the ground wet or is it dry? Is the grass thick or is it cut? Is the field choppy or flat? These different factors can change the way outfielders and in-fielders attack baseballs.

130. Visualization

Some players who are very in-tune with the mind to body con-nection use visualization the night before a game or a few hours before the game. Visualization is physically seeing yourself per-form in the game you are about to play and envisioning success. For visualization to work the best, the player must be in a quiet environment and take in the entire setting. Taking 15 minutes to sit in a quiet room and visualize yourself being successful in this upcoming game could be just the trick that moves you from good to great. Therefore, it is important as a freshman that you look up what the fields look like if you are going to visualize effectively. Physically close your eyes and look into the stands and the dug-out. By envisioning yourself in that setting and being successful you are more likely to be successful than if you do not visualize or are not prepared or comfortable in the new environment.

131. Fun

Don't lose sight of the fun in college baseball or feel overwhelmed by this book. Yes the game can be very taxing and difficult mentally and physically, but it is worth it if you love the game and are having fun. This is the reason you chose to stick with baseball for this long and to play in college. If you play a full season of college baseball you too will get the experience of a lifetime and have enough memories and stories to last a lifetime.

CPSIA information can be obtained
at www.ICGtesting.com
Printed in the USA
LVHW081504230321
682224LV00055BA/1633

9 781480 983656